Retrievers

Laura K. Murray

CREATIVE EDUCATION • CREATIVE PAPERBACKS

seedlings

Published by Creative Education and Creative Paperbacks
P.O. Box 227, Mankato, Minnesota 56002
Creative Education and Creative Paperbacks
are imprints of The Creative Company
www.thecreativecompany.us

Design by Ellen Huber; production by Travis Green
Art direction by Rita Marshall
Printed in the United States of America

Photographs by Corbis (Mark Raycroft/Minden Pictures),
Dreamstime (Adogslifephoto, Amidala76, Margarita Borodina,
Waldemar Dabrowski, Tommy Maenhout, Onetouchspark,
Jens Stolt, Bertold Werkmann), Getty Images (Betty Wiley),
iStockphoto (Jon Huelskamp), Shutterstock (Erkki Alvenmod,
Russ Beinder, Volodymyr Burdiak, Firelia, HardheadMonster,
usanee hirata, Eric Isselee, Viorel Sima), SuperStock (Minden
Pictures)

Library of Congress Cataloging-in-Publication Data
Murray, Laura K.
Retrievers / Laura K. Murray.
p. cm. — (Seedlings)
Includes bibliographical references and index.
Summary: A kindergarten-level introduction to retrievers,
covering their personalities, behaviors, life span, and such
defining features as their coats.
ISBN 978-1-60818-664-8 (hardcover)
ISBN 978-1-62832-249-1 (pbk)
ISBN 978-1-56660-678-3 (eBook)
1. Retrievers—Juvenile literature. 2. Dog breeds—Juvenile
literature. I. Title. II. Series: Seedlings.
SF429.R4M87 2016
636.752'7—dc23   2015007565

CCSS: RI.K.1, 2, 3, 4, 5, 6, 7; RI.1.1,
2, 3, 4, 5, 6, 7; RF.K.1, 3; RF.1.1

First Edition HC 9 8 7 6 5 4 3 2 1
First Edition PBK 9 8 7 6 5 4 3 2 1

TABLE OF CONTENTS

Hello,
retrievers!

Retrievers
are breeds of
friendly dogs.

They find things and
bring them back.

A retriever uses its nose to help! It finds people who are lost.

It goes hunting for birds, too.

Retrievers are large dogs.

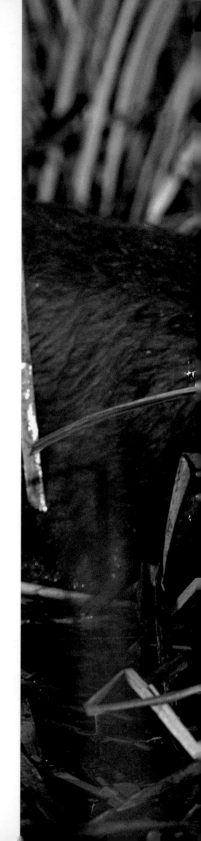

Chesapeake Bay retrievers can weigh 80 pounds!

Labrador retrievers have short hair. Golden retrievers have long hair.

Dogs shed hair
to keep their
coat healthy.

Retriever puppies have sharp nails and teeth. They need to be trained.

A pet retriever can live for 10 to 15 years.

Retrievers play fetch outside. They jump in the water.

Then they take
a nap.

Goodbye, retrievers!

Picture a Retriever

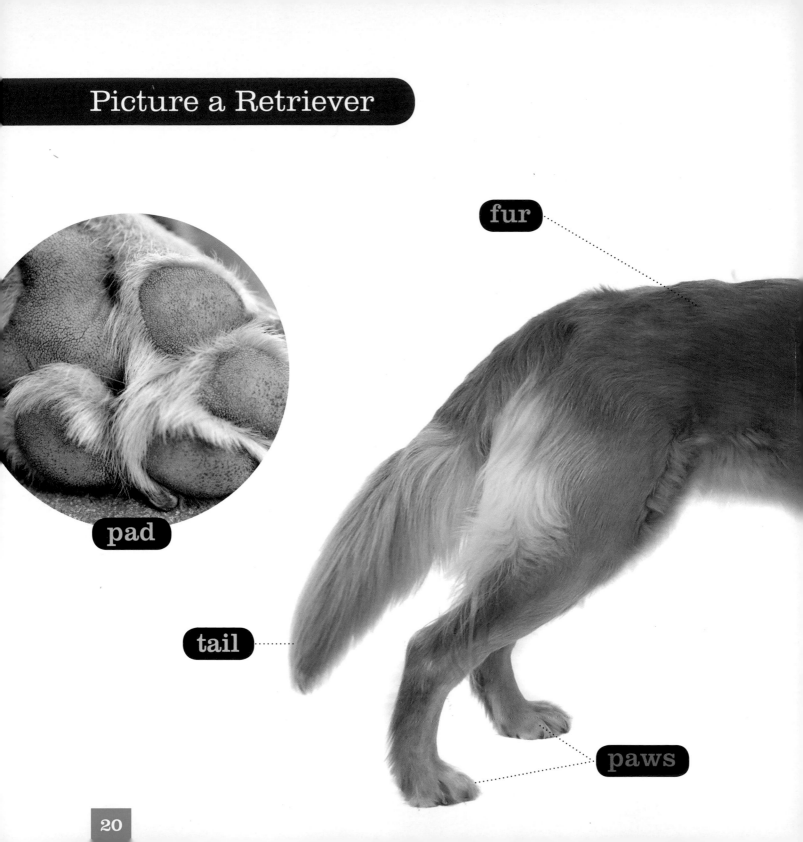

fur

pad

tail

paws

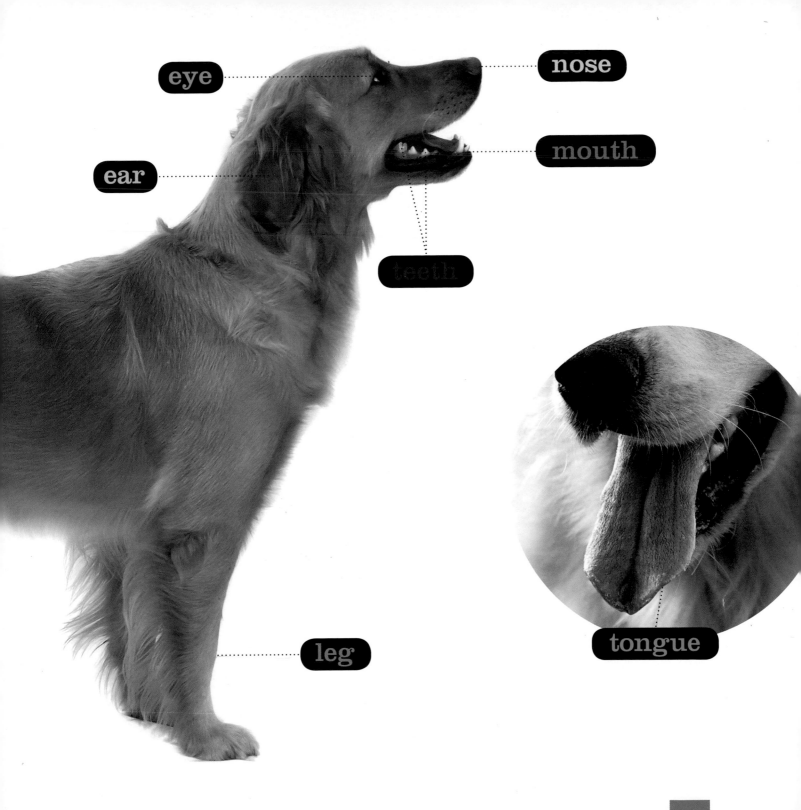

eye

nose

ear

mouth

teeth

leg

tongue

Words to Know

breeds: groups of dogs that are alike

coat: the fur or hair of an animal

shed: to get rid of

trained: to have actions changed; dogs are trained to listen to their owners

Read More

Johnson, Jinny. *Labrador Retriever*.
Mankato, Minn.: Smart Apple Media, 2013.

Schuh, Mari. *Golden Retrievers*.
Minneapolis: Bellwether Media, 2009.

Websites

Bailey's Responsible Dog Owner's Coloring Book
https://images.akc.org/pdf/public_education
/coloring_book.pdf
Print out pictures of pet dogs to color.

Labrador Retriever Video
http://www.animalplanet.com/tv-shows/dogs-101
Watch videos about retrievers and other dogs.

Index

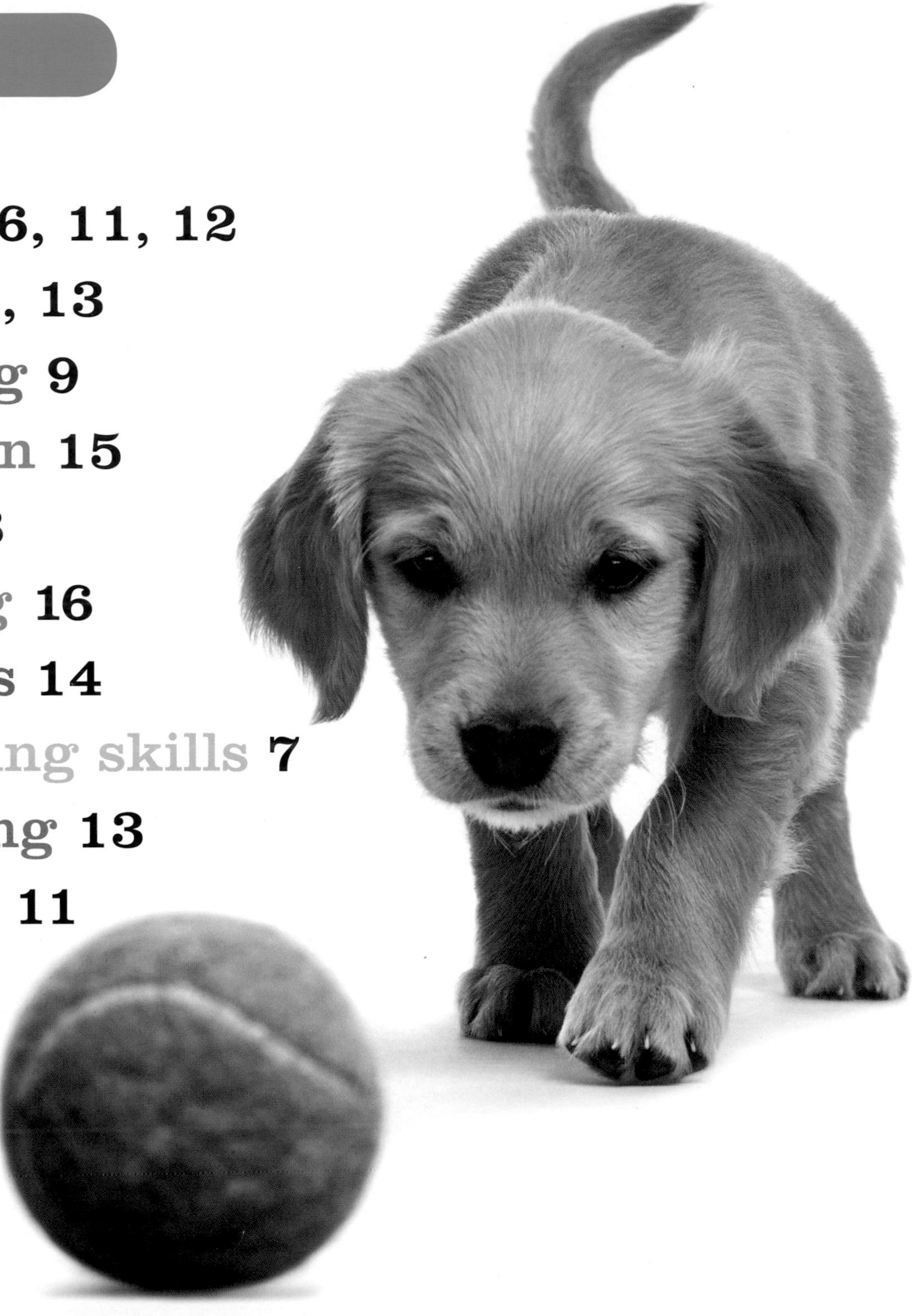